I0476316

DEBT FREE

13 Must Know Debt Management Strategies to Get Out of Debt Fast and Finally Have Financial Freedom

Michael Henson

© 2015 Sender Publishing

© Copyright 2015 by Sender Publishing — All rights reserved.

This document is geared towards providing exact and reliable information in regards to the topic and issue covered. The publication is sold with the idea that the publisher is not required to render accounting, officially permitted, or otherwise, qualified services. If advice is necessary, legal or professional, a practiced individual in the profession should be ordered.

From a Declaration of Principles which was accepted and approved equally by a Committee of the American Bar Association and a Committee of Publishers and Associations.

In no way is it legal to reproduce, duplicate, or transmit any part of this document in either electronic means or in printed format. Recording of this publication is strictly prohibited and any storage of this document is not allowed unless with written permission from the publisher. All rights reserved.

The information provided herein is stated to be truthful and consistent, in that any liability, in terms of inattention or otherwise, by any usage or abuse of any policies, processes, or directions contained within is the solitary and utter responsibility of the recipient reader. Under no circumstances will any legal responsibility or blame be held against the publisher for any reparation, damages, or monetary loss due to the information herein, either directly or indirectly.

Respective authors own all copyrights not held by the publisher.

The information herein is offered for informational purposes solely, and is universal as so. The presentation of the information is without contract or any type of guarantee assurance.

The trademarks that are used are without any consent, and the publication of the trademark is without permission or backing by the trademark owner. All trademarks and brands within this book are for clarifying purposes only and are owned by the owners themselves, not affiliated with this document.

Table of Contents

INTRODUCTION

They say money can't buy you happiness, but also that it is a necessary evil. You need money to pay your basic living expenses. You also need money to enjoy anything extra. Starting out on your own can be scary if you don't have enough money.

The days and the years go by quickly, and most people don't have enough money saved for retirement. Even if they have made a decent income, they don't have much leftover. It can be an uneasy feeling to have a large amount of debt hanging over you at any age.

It is also hard to get out of debt once you are in such a predicament. The laws have changed drastically relating to bankruptcy, too. You can't just get all of your debts wiped away as one might think. If you do file for bankruptcy, it will stay on your credit report for at least 10 years.

This is going to make it extremely difficult for you to obtain any type of credit in the future. You won't be able to get such credit without a co-signer and without high interest rates.

No matter how old you are or how much you owe, you can use the strategies in this book to help you get out of debt. It will be a delightful feeling to keep your money when you earn it, instead of paying it all towards debt.

Some of us spend unwisely and it finally catches up to us. For example, buying on credit now and then paying for it later. Even worse, some people no longer use the items they are still paying for.

For others, debts occur due to circumstances. Perhaps you had to take out large amounts of student loans to attend college. Perhaps your marriage didn't work out and you had quite a bit of debt to carry on your own after a divorce. Starting over is never easy and it can prove to be very expensive.

Medical expenses can add up quickly when you don't have money put away. Even if you have decent health insurance coverage, the costs you pay out of pocket can add up quickly.

The economy also plays a role in debt for those who have lost their jobs. Living off of credit cards and any cash in savings is all too common. They can hope to get a job soon, but in the meantime they do what they can to survive.

Society also manipulates and tricks us into thinking debt is acceptable. Having a nice home, expensive cars, and designer clothing is all part of one's overall image. Marketing is intentionally designed to motivate us to spend.

Very few people have the cash to buy big ticket items outright. Yet financing makes it possible to spread the payments out over many years. With a home, for example, you can have a mortgage that lasts 30 years.

Making minimum payments on credit cards and other debt can seem ideal. After all, you don't have to pay out a lump sum. It is only when you carefully crunch the numbers and add in the interest that you see just how much that convenience is actually costing you.

Stop putting money into the pockets of your creditors! Now is the time to pay them off and keep that money in your own accounts. You can save it, you can invest it, and you can use it to pay off one debt after another until you are down to just the monthly obligations and necessities to pay.

No matter what the circumstances are that led you down a path of debt, it is time to erase it. Don't let guilt or anger eat away at you. It is time to make some positive changes and to see the dollar amount you owe decrease.

It is going to take a plan of action and plenty of discipline. It is going to take evaluating wants versus needs. It is also going to take working hard and understanding the best way to allocate the money you have to pay off higher-interest debts first.

As you read this book, you will be able to identify ways you can eliminate your debt. I encourage you to stop after each chapter and write down the steps you can take that will get you closer to your ultimate goal of being debt free.

CHAPTER 1
Talking to Your Partner

Money concerns are the number one cause of stress and fighting in a partnership. Having money discussions are important: they should be part of the communication before living together, before marriage, and while making a life together. Both partners should play a role in budgeting and maintaining the household finances.

Debt denial can be tough to overcome for any individual. When you have two people in a given household, it is important they are on the same page financially. When we fall in love, we think about all the many reasons to spend forever with that special someone. Finances usually aren't on that list.

However, it is unrealistic to believe you can make the relationship work if you aren't on the same page when it comes to money matters. In some households, one person is a spender and the other is a saver. This can result in plenty of head-butting.

It can result in the saver being very resentful of the spender. It can also result in the spender hiding purchases and sneaking around to cover up how much things cost. This isn't good behavior for any relationship.

In many households, both parties aren't making the best decisions about spending or saving. They may be just barely getting by and when something comes along—such as an emergency expense—they panic.

When disaster strikes, people will do all they can to come up with the money. This can result in poor choices, such as payday loans with ridiculously high interest. It can also result in using credit cards with high interest rates for cash advances. Talking to your partner and working as a team to erase debt is important.

Why It Matters

You may be saying, *so what if we have debt? Everyone we know does too!* This can include your friends, family, and co-workers. Therefore, you and your partner may have the same idea about it. You may think it is normal to be in debt.

Sadly, being in debt is all too common in our society. Approximately 50% of all households in the USA are living beyond their means month after month. They are carrying credit card debt and other debts that eat up at least 80% of their monthly income.

Paying only the minimum amount due each month isn't enough to take care of the problem. It isn't enough to reduce the debt. In fact, interest accumulates so quickly that your minimum payment is usually barely scratching the surface of that debt.

The average household in the USA with credit card debt owes approximately $14,000! However, these are also the same people buying fancy coffees each morning, getting the latest smartphone on their cell plans, and upgrading their TV this weekend.

You and your partner have to treat debt like the enemy. You have to decide to make it a priority for your future. It can be unpleasant at first to talk about debt. However, you both need to be honest and you both need to be fair.

Talking about debt isn't a time for the blame game. It isn't a time to decide who caused what debt and why it shouldn't have happened. If only one of you works or one makes more than the other, this shouldn't be an issue either.

You are a team and what you do financially as a unit and individually affects your entire household. You can't make a difference in your debt if you are against each other. Be willing to come up with a plan you can both stick to without being resentful.

Establish a time when you can both talk about debt without interruptions. Try to do so early in the day so you aren't tired and disconnected. Focus on the ultimate goal and encourage each other to take steps that will help you to reach such goals.

Once you get your initial plan of action in place, schedule a time to talk about debt once a month. Put it on the calendar so you don't forget. If you need to modify your plan of action, it is fine to do so. Just don't give up!

CHAPTER 2
Changing Your Mindset

If your mindset has always been "it is fine to buy now and pay later," you need to end it. Are you still paying for a trip you took to Las Vegas three years ago? Do you feel like you owe more and more all the time without seeing signs that your payments are making a dent?

It is time to change the way you think about spending. This can be tough, but you have to be disciplined. You also have to be honest with yourself. Why do you spend the way you do? Are you trying to impress your peers?

Do you feel you need to have the best of everything due to emotional concerns? Some people shop because they are unhappy and the spending actually gives them a rush of adrenaline that feels good. The problem is that they later feel guilty about spending. This guilt leads to negative feelings and the cycle repeats again and again. They aren't addressing the root of the problem. If this sounds like you, it may be time to seek some professional help. At the very least, you may wish to talk to a credit counselor.

You may feel like your debt is a dark cloud that follows you everywhere. Maybe you have debt collectors calling and you choose not to answer your phone. Avoiding the problem though isn't going to make it go away.

If you have other vices that cost you plenty of money, then you need to deal with those issues. For example, the amount of money spent on pornography, gambling, drinking and/or drugs can quickly become too much. It is important that you eliminate those issues from your life. There is professional help and care available to assist you.

Maybe part of the problem is you simply don't make enough money. Check to see if you and your family qualify for any government programs available. This can include:

- Medical Care Assistance
- Food Stamps
- Cash Payments from the State
- Housing and Utility Assistance
- Tuition Assistance

If you had to borrow lots of money to complete college, you may feel overwhelmed. You just barely got out of college and found a job. Now you have a mountain of debt to get through. Find out if you qualify for any debt forgiveness programs.

If you are employed in certain types of work in a low income area, you may be able to get a percentage of those loans reduced. For example, if you work in the medical field, social work, or education, it is certainly worth looking in to.

The military reserves can also offer you a chance to change your situation. They help with discipline and self-esteem, while you earn money. You may be able to get assistance with paying what you owe for college, too.

There are plenty of ways to find out about programs that will assist you. Find out what the specific requirements are and how you apply. Provide any documentation they request so your application can be processed. Such help is out there, and it may be a way for you to reduce your debt and improve your feelings about it.

If you spend money to try to keep up appearances, let it go. Chances are those around you do the same thing. They may have more stuff, but you are going to be happier. You will be able to go to sleep at night without worry about money down the road.

Some parents spend a ton of money on their kids—trying to give them everything they didn't have. It is important to make sure kids have their basic needs met. Yet, it is unrealistic to think they need every new gadget that comes out or only name-brand clothing.

When children are given everything, they appreciate even less. It is fine to give your children gifts and to have some extras for them. Just make sure you have boundaries in place and you aren't catering to an unrealistic lifestyle.

Don't think about not spending money as a punishment. Think of it as a challenge! Discover new ways you can have fun without spending lots of money. As you develop these new habits, you will find you are less and less inclined to spend money on things you don't really need.

CHAPTER 3
Understanding Needs
Versus Wants

Marketing techniques are very clever in the way they appeal to the senses. There is research that indicates our subconscious picks up a great deal we aren't aware of. This can then drive our purchasing decisions.

Understanding "needs versus wants" may seem like a fairly easy concept when you think of it. Yet as you dig into it, you will realize it isn't just black and white.

Needs

Items we all must have to survive are considered to be needs. This includes:

- Food
- Water
- Shelter
- Clothing
- Hygiene products
- Transportation

Wants

Items you would love to have but you don't need are wants. This can include:

- Mobile phone
- Cable
- Dishwasher

Wants are things we desire and they can be very appealing to us. Perhaps it is something that tastes great such as eating out instead of eating at home.

Maybe you really want that pair of shoes in the window you walk by each day before work. They aren't a necessity but you already know they would look amazing with a certain outfit in your closet!

We already said food and clothing are necessities . . . so why are they listed as wants too? This is where it all starts to get complicated. You do need food, but you don't need a $60 dinner for two. You need clothing, but you don't need $100 shoes to go with one outfit.

Transportation is also a big one. Sure, you may need a car to successfully get around. You may need it to commute to work, to get kids to activities, and even to go to the grocery store. However, you don't need a brand new, upscale, luxury SUV!

Emotions

Our emotions can drive us to buy certain wants when we could live without them. Many women will tell you they love the confidence certain cosmetics give them. They wouldn't dream of cutting them out of the household budget!

There are some women who will only wear a certain brand of jeans. They like the way their body looks in them and this gives them confidence. They may have tried other jeans that cost less but they don't fit as well.

It is fine to treat ourselves to something now and then, but when this gets to be excessive, we get into trouble. Most households aren't experiencing debt due to a few minor purchases. It is the result of chronic purchases again and again. The amount they owe continues to climb.

Logic

You have to allow logic to rule the game. Suppose you aren't willing to give up your cosmetics, so that stays in the budget. As a compromise, however, you would be willing to make your own coffee at home rather than buying a $2 cup on the way to work each day ($40 per month).

You may be willing to allow yourself two pairs of the great-looking, expensive jeans you like so much. The compromise can be to buy a few other pairs of less expensive ones and only to wear the expensive ones on days when you have a good reason.

Time

Needs versus wants often comes to mind when time is the issue. For example, some households eat out several times a week. This is far more expensive than the cost of going to the grocery store and buying food to make meals.

However, the parents feel they simply don't have time for shopping and preparing meals every single day. You have to find ways to balance your time to make it all fit. One suggestion is to make larger portions and eat the left-overs the next day, so you only have to cook every-other night.

Evaluate Before You Buy

Always evaluate a product before you buy it. The actual product itself may be a need. However, all the extra perks it comes with can be wants. For example, you may decide that you need a mobile phone for work and emergencies. You can get a basic phone for a decent price per month. You may even be able to get the phone for free based on promotions. However, they will try to sell you the most advanced mobile phone available and plenty of perks.

Going with the latter option is going to cost you more both for the service and for the phone. As a result, you fulfill the actual need, but you are spending so much more due to the want. That $25 per month they charge you for phone service adds up to $300 per year, while a pay-as-you-go plan can cost only a fraction of that.

CHAPTER 4
Understanding Interest Rates

Any time you buy something on credit, you will pay interest. Your goal should always be to pay the least amount of interest possible. When you can, save up the entire cost before you buy something. Then you won't pay any interest at all.

This isn't always possible, however, so you have to be a smart and savvy consumer. Some types of loans have a given rate of interest across the board. This includes payday loans, which are never recommended for a cash advance due to the high costs!

What Determines Interest Rates?

Most of the time, the interest rate will be a variable. The lender will input all of your information and a formula is used to decide what they can offer you.

Too few consumers realize that if they don't like what is offered, they don't have to accept it. They can decline the credit and move on. Your credit score will take a hit if you have too many credit inquiries.

With that in mind, do your homework before you apply. Look for the best lenders and the best rates of interest. The proposed rate of interest depends on many factors. They include:

- Lenders
- Economy
- Collateral (or not)
- Type of purchase
- Credit history
- Credit score

With this in mind, you have to see what the interest is going to be for the purchase. The higher the interest is, the more you will pay for the item when all is said and done.

Even a 1% difference in interest can be thousands of dollars more you pay on that debt. Your goal should be to finance only what you must and only for the lowest amount you have to. You should also find a lender offering the lowest amount of interest.

If you don't have any credit, it is hard to get credit. Yet once you acquire it, the lenders seem to come out of the woodwork. You get new credit card offers all the time. When you check out at a department store, they may ask if you want to apply for a credit card to get a discount on that purchase.

Limit what you apply for as the more credit you have, the lower your credit score will be. You are seen as a higher risk to the lenders and that can boost your interest rate when you do decide to buy something on credit.

Special Promotions

There are special promotions out there that can work to your advantage. However, this is only the case if you pay attention and look out for them. For example, you may be offered 0% interest for 6 months. If you pay the full balance in that 6 months, there is no interest and it is the same as a cash purchase.

However, if you don't completely pay it off in 6 months, interest is applied. That amount of interest is typically going to be in the double digits. This is far too much to pay for credit, and so you need to only accept such an offer if you know you can pay it off in the six month timeframe.

See More Than the Monthly Payment

Pay attention to the overall interest you will pay for something, not just the monthly payment. Don't get tunnel vision and just see that they will only require you to pay $40 per month for that big screen TV you want!

You will be paying $40 a month for many years on it. When you add together that payment amount with all of the interest, it is an astonishing amount of money you will pay in total. Far more than the value of the TV.

Pre-Payment Penalties

While your goal should always be to pay off debt as quickly as you can, there are some lenders that will actually penalize you for doing so. Make sure your read all the terms and conditions so you can avoid these types of predators.

Should you pay off what you owe them early, they have the right to add on fees and other costs. This is referred to as a pre-payment penalty. If consumers would stop borrowing from them, such lenders would have no choice but to change these awful methods.

Free Calculator Tools Online

Seeing the big picture is the key to understanding interest rates. Use free online calculator tools to help you determine this information. Just enter the amount you will borrow, the interest rate, and the monthly payment.

It will tell you what the overall cost of that purchase is going to be. When you see that figure, then you can determine if it's worth the value or not. Most of the time, you will avoid borrowing once you see that figure!

CHAPTER 5
Evaluating Your Income and Spending

Too often, consumers think that if they only had more money, they could pay their bills and be fine. Yet it is the spending habits themselves that must change. Otherwise, you may earn more money but you will also spend more. You may upgrade your vehicle and your house. You may buy items on credit that you wouldn't have before. So you have a larger income, but now you also have far more expenses.

Never refinance your home in order to receive money unless you apply it all towards your debt. At the same time, you have to decide not to incur any more debt that isn't a necessity. If you continue your same spending habits, you will rack up debt again very quickly.

You'll also have that second mortgage payment to think about now. Or you may have lost all of the equity in your home and must now start over with the payments and interest over the next 30 years.

Write Down All Income

To get a very good indication of your income and expenses, you need to write it all down. Do you ever look at your checking account and wonder where all your money went? Do you ever get upset that you make good money but have nothing left by the time your next pay day rolls around?

You aren't alone with this, and that is why learning about your income and spending is so important. Your income should include:

- Wages (take-home)
- Tips (lowest estimate)
- Commissions (lowest estimate)

Don't use your gross income because that isn't very accurate. By the time they take out deductions including taxes, social security, and health insurance premiums, your take-home salary is much less.

If you earn tips, you can't predict how much you will receive. You should therefore budget the lowest possible amount into the equation. If you earn more tips than you estimated that month, great news! This means you have extra money to pay towards your debt.

The same is true with commissions. If you get a base paycheck plus commission, estimate the commission on the lower side. However, you should always strive to make as much as you can with such commission offers. The more you earn, the faster you can pay off debt.

Write Down All Expenses

Next, you need to write down *all* of your expenses. Start with your basic living costs. This should include:

- Food
- Shelter
- Utilities
- Transportation (such as gas or public transport tickets)
- Car payments
- Medications

Then, write down all of your variable expenses. This should include your credit cards and other unsecured debt. The goal will be to pay this off as soon as you can.

Track it All

What people often fail to keep track of with their expenses is the smaller things. And however small, they do add up quickly. If you go out for dinner and drinks with friends every weekend, you may be spending $200 a month that you didn't even factor into your expenses.

With that in mind, your challenge is to write down everything you spend money on for the next 30 days. Your partner should be doing the same. It doesn't matter if you spend $1 for a tip or you spend $100 to pay a bill.

At the end of the 30 days, go through the list. Highlight in one color all of the necessary expenses. Highlight in another color all of the unnecessary expenses. Those are expenditures you can eliminate. With that money freed up, you can use it to pay your debt!

CHAPTER 6
Making a Budget and Sticking to It

It is amazing how many households don't have a budget in place. They're simply aware that some money is coming in and some money is going back out. This can be a stressful and chaotic cycle.

If you don't have enough money to get you from one payday to the next, you have serious budgeting issues. You are living beyond your means and you need to stop charging new expenses. It is all about to come to a screeching halt!

Write It Down

Write down all of the monthly expenses you must pay. Write down the name of the bill and the amount due. For revolving credit, write down the balance due and the minimum monthly payment.

Hopefully, your budget will enable you to pay more than just the minimum. We will cover this in a future chapter. For this chapter, it's important to get an idea of what you must pay to stay on top of your bills. It doesn't mean you are doing well, though, if you only just have your head above the water. Sooner or later, you will get tired of treading.

Variable Expenses

For variable expenses, such as groceries, you need to choose an appropriate amount and stick to it. Don't just go to the grocery store and then stress at the checkout over the amount.

Get ads from the store and see what is on sale. Buy items that are low in cost but high in nutrition. Determine a dollar amount you will spend for the week and make it work. Soups, casseroles, and other meals are low-cost, and they can feed a household more than one meal.

Divide the Remainder

The difference between your income and your expenses is what you have left. Divide this amount into four envelopes labeled:

- Savings
- Emergency Fund
- Debt-Elimination
- Spending

It is important to put money into savings, so you can build a nest egg. Even when you are trying to pay off debt, you need to put something into savings. You also need funds for emergencies. When the water heater or the refrigerator goes out, don't reach for the credit card.

Instead, go to your emergency fund. Then you can pay for what you need and without worrying about interest or more debt. Don't touch your emergency fund unless you absolutely must.

A quarter of the money should go towards eliminating your debt. It doesn't matter if that envelope holds $50 or $500 each month. The idea is you are working towards paying down your debt. Even paying $50 per month adds up to $600 annually.

The last envelop is for spending. This doesn't mean to run out and buy whatever you want! It should be used for household items that you didn't budget for. Perhaps your daughter comes home and needs $20 for a field-trip. That money comes out of the spending envelope.

Choose how you spend that money wisely—as once it is gone for that pay period, it is gone! Don't let yourself charge anything more to your credit cards, and don't borrow funds from other accounts. Spend responsibly!

CHAPTER 7
Emergency Funds

As mentioned in the previous chapter, it is important to have an emergency fund. Many people argue this point. They feel that they already don't have enough money, so why should they put more of it away for emergencies?

You may feel that you should use this money to pay for the things that have been adding up. However, there is a solid reason why you need to have an emergency fund in place: it allows you to have some control over what is taking place in your life.

When there is an emergency expense, often our first thought is *oh no, how much will that cost me? How will I come up with that amount of money in a hurry?* You may feel pressured to not make your house payment so you can pay for that emergency need.

This just creates more financial problems, however. You will now have your mortgage company calling you daily since you skipped a payment. They may also add on charges that will increase your debt. Furthermore, they will report the late payment to the credit bureaus and that can reduce your overall credit score.

Backed into a Corner

As you build an emergency fund, you will no longer feel backed into a corner. Too many people feel they have no choice in an emergency but not to pay some bills. Others will resort to high-interest credit cards that take years to pay off.

Another scenario that often plays out is people borrowing from No-credit-check! payday loans. It is so easy to walk in there with a pay-stub and a bank account statement. Depending on the location, you can get $1,000 or more in minutes. This seemingly easy interaction actually comes with a huge penalty and interest rates that are astronomical.

Since there is no credit check, every customer pays the same amount of interest for such a loan. It is around 22% to 27%, but can vary based on location and lender. They often let you pay it in small installments over time.

This then becomes one more debt you have to pay each month. The amount of interest you pay is often up to 60% of the total loan amount. For example, if you borrow $500 from a payday loan for an emergency situation, you will repay about $800 when all is said and done.

If you, instead, had that $500 in your emergency fund, it would be like getting a 0% interest loan. The $300 or so you would save in interest could be used to pay off additional debt or to restock your emergency fund.

Keep Credit Cards Open

Avoid putting emergency needs on a credit card. Once you do so, it is extremely hard to pay it off. Keep those credit cards open with as low of a balance as possible. Not only will it save you interest, it will boost your credit score.

With a higher credit score, you will be able to access credit when you need it. You will also be able to get that credit at a very low interest rate. This will result in you saving money so the cycle continues to move and flow.

Three-Month Evaluation

Every three months, evaluate your emergency fund situation. Ideally, you want to get to the point where you have enough money in that account to cover all your total necessities for three months. You never know when you may lose your job or have a medical emergency. There are plenty of scenarios where your income could suddenly stop, so you don't want to be in a panic about it.

Once you have saved enough for this three-month buffer, you should reward yourself. That is a huge accomplishment and it shouldn't go unnoticed. Spend some time doing something you love or even order a pizza! Don't spend a ton of money though!

At your three-month evaluations, you can choose to remove any funds from that account that are above and beyond that 90-day buffer. Use that money to pay down your debts. If you haven't had any emergency expenses occur, you will feel good paying a little extra towards debt now and then.

Example:
Monthly necessary expenses ($2,000) x 3 months = $6,000 in account.

Your regular evaluation shows the account has $5,800 in it. Don't take anything out to pay towards debt. At your next three-month evaluation, the account has $7,000 in it. Take $1,000 out of the account and pay it towards a debt.

CHAPTER 8
Always Pay Bills on Time

One of the main goals of having a budget and tracking your expenses and spending, is to see where the cash flow problems occur. On paper, you may make enough to pay your bills, but it isn't getting done due to the many extras.

You must get into the habit of paying your bills on time. There is *no* exception to this rule. If you want to pay off your debt, you need to allocate money wisely. A $25 late charge is a waste of your money. And a disconnect fee and reconnect charge is absolutely unnecessary.

Avoid Late Fees

Know when your bills are due so you can avoid late fees. That, combined with budgeting your money well, is important. If you pay bills online, use a debit card and not a credit card. If you mail in a payment, make sure you allow ample time for the payment to arrive.

If you do get a late fee, call and ask for it to be removed. If you have a good history with the lender, they will usually do so. If the agent says they can't, ask to talk to a supervisor.

If you are chronically late with your payments though, forget it. There is no way they can justify helping you out when you aren't doing your part.

Avoid Overdraft Fees

If you have a checking account, pay attention to the balance. Don't end up with overdraft fees. They can be $25 or more per check if they decide to cover it. Nothing is worse than owing your bank—and when you do get paid, they will get a piece of it first.

If you chronically have overdrafts, your bank will get tired of your behavior. They will start to return your checks to the payees. Then you will have overdraft fees and also fees that each payee adds on.

If you fail to pay them, they can take you to court. Many states allow you to collect up to three times the value of the check plus court costs. You don't want to wind up in such a financial mess!

Make sure you have money in the bank to pay your bills. Every time you write a check, make sure it gets put into your registry. Double-check your math too, so errors don't cause problems.

You can also round up for all of your checks. When the amount is $19.06 enter $20 into your checkbook. That little bit of change is going to add up. In the end, it may give you a small cushion in your account, which could save you from an overdraft due to a mathematical error.

Improve Credit Score

Consistently paying your bills on time will improve your credit score. A percentage of your overall score is based on your payment history. This can help if your amount of debt has resulted in a lower credit score than you would like to see.

Better Interest Rates

Paying your bills on time also allows you to get better interest rates. Lower interest can save you hundreds or even thousands of dollars annually.

Negotiate with Creditors

When you pay your bills on time, you have room to negotiate with your creditors. You can call them and ask for help if you are struggling. They may be able to defer a few payments to help get you back on track.

They may also have a repayment plan that allows you to pay less per month. The interest is either lowered or no longer accumulates on the account as long as you keep your end of the agreement.

More creditors are working with consumers than ever before. Don't be shy about talking to them. Just make sure you get the terms and conditions of the agreed upon offer in writing. And finally, be polite!

CHAPTER 9
Reducing Expenses

A huge part of your plan of action is going to be reducing your expenses. When you do so, you have more money left over to allocate towards your debts. It is amazing how much money you can save up per month by realizing where it is all going!

This is a really good time to sit down with your partner and make some decisions. It is also a time to sit down with the kids and tell them spending is about to change. Don't worry, everyone is going to survive!

Eating Out

It was mentioned in a previous chapter, but important to mention here too. The average household of 4 can spend $100 easily going out to dinner and then a movie. Yet you can rent a movie and order a pizza for about $20.

Eating at home more is a great way to cut down on expenses. Eat breakfast at home and take your lunch to work. Eat dinner at home instead of dining out.

If your family loves to eat out, make some compromises. Agree to do so once every other week instead of several times per week. Then no one feels deprived.

Gym Membership

While staying fit is important, you don't need a monthly gym membership to make it happen. This is a great time for you to reduce debt. If you pay $60 per month at the gym you can pay off $720 in debt next year. You can engage in various forms of free exercise.

Cable

The average household has more channels than you can imagine. Yet they watch very few of them. It is time to cut down that cable package to just the bare minimum. You can also decide to cut it out completely.

Shop Around

If you are going to buy something, do your homework to get it for the lowest possible price. If you shop online, look for promo codes such as % off and free shipping. Never pay full price if you don't have to. You can also consider used items instead of new when possible.

Trade Services

Find other people you can trade services with to reduce expenses. I have a friend who cuts our hair for free. In exchange, I pick up her kids after school each day and watch them for 1 ½ hours. She doesn't have to pay for child care and I don't have to pay for expensive haircuts.

Car Pool

You can slash your cost of fuel in half by commuting to and from work with someone else. You can also reduce the wear and tear on your vehicle this way. Depending on where you live, public transportation may be an inexpensive option.

Insurance Policies

Always take the time to evaluate insurance policies. Your home and your vehicles should be combined to get you discounts. Your deductible should be looked at too. If it is $500, make sure you can cover that in your emergency fund. If you up it to $750, you may be able to save on your monthly premiums.

Trade in the Car

If you have an expensive car, trade it in. Get something that is more efficient in terms of gas. Look for a vehicle that gets lower rates for insurance too.

Heating and Cooling

Keep your heating and cooling settings on a certain temperature. If household members get hot they can dress lightly and open windows. If they get cold they can put on a sweater or get a blanket.

CHAPTER 10
Making More Money

While you are working hard to reduce expenses, you should also think about ways to make more money! This can be a double win that many people don't see until it is pointed out to them.

For example, let's say you reduce your monthly expenses by $400. Then you increase your income by $300 per month. Now you have an additional $700 each month that you can use to reduce your debt! Think about how powerful that is going to be!

Sell What You Don't Need

Go through your home one room at a time. Remove anything you don't use. Get rid of clothing you no longer wear. You will love the de-cluttering process. At the same time, you can make money selling what you don't need.

You can have a yard sale or you can post items online on craigslist or eBay for example. Use any money you make selling these items to pay off your debt. You may be surprised at just how much you can earn this way.

Work Overtime

If your boss allows it, work overtime when you can. This is extra money you can earn and use. It also takes up some of your free time, which means you won't be spending money.

Let it be known that you are willing to work late or to pick up extra shifts. Your boss will appreciate the effort and it may earn you a promotion down the road.

Be willing to work on weekends and holidays if there is extra pay involved. You may be able to earn time-and-a-half for such occasions. This is an easy way to earn extra money.

Get a Second Job

Think about getting a second job. This is ideal around the holidays when many retailers are hiring seasonal help. You can also get a weekend job if you are typically off those days.

Offer services such as lawn care or babysitting. Perhaps you have some handyman skills that others would find helpful. You can spend your time helping them and, at the same time, you can make some great money.

Referrals and Incentives

Find out about any types of referrals and incentives offered at your job. If you work on commission, come up with new ways to reach clients and to generate more sales. Make sure you work hard to develop relationships, too, for repeat customers and purchases.

Perhaps there are contests to help motivate you. Do your best to win them so you can get those perks and incentives. Maybe there are bonuses offered at work if you meet certain goals. Tap into your full potential to earn them!

CHAPTER 11
Allocating Extra Money To Pay Down Your Debt

Now that you are in control of your money, you will start to see the rewards from it. You can see that extra money going to pay down your debt.

Create a Spreadsheet

It is a good idea to create a spreadsheet. This is an easy way to see your information at a glance. It also allows you to track your progress. Such data is important as it will help you to stay motivated and to continue paying off debts.

You can write down the information by hand, but you will find that a spreadsheet allows you to get more done in less time and will even do some of the math for you. Your spreadsheet needs to include:

- Creditor name
- Balance due
- Minimum monthly payment
- Interest rate

Once you have everything listed, arrange it with the highest-interest debt at the top. Continue in this sequence to the lowest interest rate. Too often, people list them by the lowest debt amount to the highest, but that isn't as effective.

Stacking or Rolling

By paying off your debts with the highest interest first, you save more money overall. As you pay off a debt, you can put that monthly money towards the next highest interest rate.

This process is called stacking or rolling. The idea is to take the funds you used to pay on a given debt and then allocate it to the next. The more you pay off, the more you have to work with. It will usually take you longer to pay off the first debt than the rest due to this method, but don't worry—you're doing it correctly.

For example, your highest interest-rate debt is $2,700 and you are paying $50 per month on it right now. Once you increase your income and reduce other spending, however, you are able to pay $450 per month.

At the same time, you are paying what is due each month on all accounts (and paying them on time)! Once this debt is paid off, you will move to the next one on your list.

Let's say you owe $3,000 on this credit card debt and you have been paying $40 per month. Now that the previous debt is paid off, you can then allocate that $450 to it for a monthly payment of $490. It will just be a matter of months before that second debt is paid off.

Reduce Interest Rates

While you are using this method to pay off debt, make sure you don't incur additional debt that isn't necessary. Your credit score should improve when your bills are paid on time and the amounts you owe are lessening.

This is an ideal time to contact creditors and ask them if they can lower your interest rates. Even if they reduce it just by a few points, it is still going to lessen the overall amount you owe them.

You can also consider transferring credit card balances to a credit card with a 0% interest rate. These types of transfers only work well, though, if you pay the debt off in full before that introductory time period ends.

Extra Funds

Make sure any extra funds you get aren't used irresponsibly. If you get a tax return, birthday money, or a work bonus, think about the best ways to use that money. Put some in savings and some of it into your emergency fund.

This can be a time to go out for a nice dinner or treat the family to an outing for the day. However, the rest of that extra money though should be used for paying off your debts. It may not be as much fun, but it sure does make a huge difference for your future.

CHAPTER 12
Keeping Good Records

It is very important that you keep good records. This is the only way to really see the progress of your efforts. Your spreadsheet can have as many columns as you'd like for keeping track of things.

Set Goals

While your overall goal is to eliminate debt, that can take many years to accomplish. That time is going to pass anyway, and you don't want to be in worse financial shape than you are at this moment.

Set goals for the short term so you can see your progress. For example, you can say that, within three months, you want to pay off a given bill. You could also say that within six months, you want your total debt to be reduced by a given amount

Evaluate Goals

Hold yourself and your partner accountable for the goals you have set. If you achieve them, praise your good efforts. If you don't, identify what isn't working. Make a plan that changes things up and allows you to continue moving forward.

Good records help you to see how much you have paid off over a given period of time. This is important as it can help you see your efforts are working well. It can also help you decide to change things if the debt isn't disappearing as quickly as you would like.

Keep Receipts

Always keep receipts when you make payments. It is awful when you think you have something paid off but the company disagrees. Keep receipts for several years so you can prove you've paid.

A pile of receipts, though, aren't going to help you. Keep an envelope for each type of bill you're paying off. On the front of it, write the starting balance as of today. Then, continue to write each date and payment amount. Put the receipt for each payment for that account into that envelope.

Such a system makes it so easy for you to stay on top of things. If you need to find a certain receipt this way, you can find it quickly and easily. If you pay bills online, print out receipts so you have a physical record.

Get Offers in Writing

Any time you negotiate interest rates or other details with a creditor, get it in writing. You should document who you talked to and when until you get such details. They can send you a letter or an email to confirm.

Document What You Pay Off

As you pay off debts, don't wipe them off your spreadsheet. Instead, document what you pay and when. This is a visual aid to keep you motivated. When you get frustrated with the debt that still remains, this spreadsheet can help you to see just how far you have come.

Check Your Credit Reports

Even though you have documents of accounts being paid, your credit reports could still be wrong. Check all three credit reporting agencies every six months. If you see discrepancies, follow their procedures to get them cleared up.

If you have bad debts that you continue to pay, they will still show up on your credit report. Make sure they reflect as being paid, though. That will help some. In time, you will be able to see overall improvements to your credit score.

Write-Off Accounts

Sometimes, a creditor will agree to allow you to pay back a portion of what you actually owe them. For example, you owe $7,000 on the credit card but they will put you on a payment plan where you can pay it off in two years.

No more interest will accumulate, but you can't use that card anymore either. It is going to be a closed account. The amount they agree to write off on your behalf is going to be reported to the IRS if it is over $600.

You will get a form called a 1099 which is for "Cancellation of Debt." You will need to include the dollar amount that was written off on your federal tax return. Doing so can increase the amount you owe the IRS or reduce the amount of return you get from the IRS.

Make sure you report such information, though, so you don't get contacted by the IRS down the road. You will have to complete an "Insolvency Worksheet" with your taxes that shows your debts were high at the time.

As long as you do this, they won't question the write-off. Many creditors feel it is to their benefit to get you to pay 60% or so of the debt and write off the rest. That way, they don't spend extra money on collections and other fees that may add up quickly for them.

CHAPTER 13
Rewarding Your Efforts

Your hard work, time, and efforts to reduce your debt does matter! Make sure you reward yourself for that work and dedication. Your rewards shouldn't be all about spending, however, you can think about making a special purchase (with cash) when you meet milestone goals.

Maybe you gave up going to your favorite place for lunch several days a week. Now you pack your lunch and save money. When you reach a given goal, allow yourself to go there and have lunch as a special treat. It doesn't have to be expensive, but it will really be rewarding.

Personalize It

You and your partner can both have your own rewards in place. You can choose individual rewards or you can choose to do something as a couple. It depends on what will continue to motivate you to keep up the good work.

For such rewards to work, they have to be personal and have meaning to you. Maybe you just want a guilt-free day to lounge around with a good book and a bubble bath. Your partner can agree to keep the kids busy for the afternoon.

What motivates you may not motivate your partner so keep that in mind. Rewards can also be for the entire family. If you have older kids, let them be part of the process involved for reducing debt. You will be sharing valuable life skills with them at the same time.

Honesty

Be honest though, and if you didn't really meet the goal then don't seek the reward. We have a way of justifying such things in our own minds to get what we want! Hold yourself (and your partner) to higher standards!

Rewards Jar

It can be fun to create a rewards jar, too. Any time you or your spouse thinks about something as a reward, write it on a slip of paper. Place it into a jar. When you reach a goal, pick one out of the jar and read it. That is what you get!

CONCLUSION

Getting into debt is too easy in today's society. However, that doesn't mean you have to continue down that path. Now that you have the right information, you can use these thirteen concepts to assist you in eliminating your debt. You can also avoid the common pitfalls that keep people trapped.

It may not be all fun and games when you are reducing your debt, but the work pays off in the end. With the right mindset and the right plan of action, you can make it happen. Your debt can be paid off, and you will be able to relax about money.

You will also be able to have more money to use for the things you want in the future. After you get your debts paid off, you may be down to only your mortgage. But it can take 30 years to pay off a house, and the amount of interest can be very high.

You can reduce years off of your mortgage loan just by paying a larger amount now and then. You can also continue to use extra funds from your emergency account to pay off your home.

Or maybe you haven't bought a home yet due to debt. By getting that current debt off the table, you can increase the dollar amount of a home that you qualify for. You can also get your home loan with a lower interest rate. The power is in your hands—not that of the lenders—when you have good credit and a low debt amount.

If you have a significant other, it is essential the two of you work out your differences about how to handle money. It is also important that both of you handle the money situation for the household. That ensures one person isn't dealing with stress over money while the other thinks it is okay to spend mindlessly.

Spending time in a debt workshop or talking with a debt counselor can help you both to see the big picture. They can also help you with setting a budget.

Once your debts are paid, you will have the luxury of paying cash for things you want. This can include going on a vacation, buying new furniture, or even saving up to get a new car. The idea is to avoid buying on credit whenever possible.

Credit can be convenient, but it is also expensive. Don't fool yourself into thinking lenders are trying to help you out. They know ultimately that they will make a fortune off of interest. This is why they offer you in-house financing. This is why credit cards are available.

There *will* be times when you need to use your credit card or other forms of credit. Just make sure that what you use them for are needs and not wants. Being disciplined about your spending habits will make it easier for you to pay off debts.

Focus on how you can earn more money and at the same time reduce your expenses. Every single dollar you free up to use towards your debt will add up quickly. Make sure you have some rewards in place too so you don't get discouraged.

Today is the day you make a decision to change things once and for all. A year from now you can have more debt, the same amount of debt, or less debt. What is the result going to be? Challenge yourself to make sacrifices now that will help you have better finances in the future.

Money can't buy you happiness but successfully managing your money certainly helps! It gives you freedom, too, so you aren't seeing your money go right back out the moment you get your paycheck. It can reduce stress and help you to have a better future in terms of financial stability.

DID YOU LIKE *"DEBT FREE?"*

Before you go, I'd like to say thank you so much for purchasing my book.

I know you could have picked from dozens of books on this subject, but you took a chance with mine, and I'm truly grateful for that.

So, once again, a big thanks for downloading this book and reading all the way to the end—I truly appreciate it.

Now I'd like to ask for a small favor if you don't mind:

Would you be so kind as to take a minute of your time and leave a review for this book on Amazon?

This feedback will help me continue to write the kind of books that help you get results. And if you loved it, then please feel free to let me know! :)

MORE BOOKS BY MICHAEL HENSON:

Investing For Beginners: 9 Little Known Investing Strategies To Help You Grow Your Money Effortlessly For Financial Freedom

Morning Ritual Secrets: 12 Simple and Easy Techniques to Help You Wake Up Motivated, Productive and Achieve Your Goals!

Meditation For Beginners: The Ultimate Beginner Meditation Guide To Help Quiet The Mind, Relieve Stress, Feel Happier and Have More Success With Mindfulness Meditation

www.ingramcontent.com/pod-product-compliance
Lightning Source LLC
Chambersburg PA
CBHW071004180526
45168CB00003B/1284